All About America

A NATION OF IMMIGRANTS

Paul Robert Walker

KINGFISHER
NEW YORK

KINGFISHER
LONDON & NEW YORK

Copyright © Bender Richardson White 2012

Published in the United States by Kingfisher,
175 Fifth Ave., New York, NY 10010
Kingfisher is an imprint of
Macmillan Children's Books, London.
All rights reserved.

Distributed in the U.S. and Canada by Macmillan,
175 Fifth Ave., New York, NY 10010

Library of Congress Cataloging-in-Publication data has been applied for.
ISBN paperback 978-0-7534-6671-1
ISBN reinforced library binding 978-0-7534-6713-8

Kingfisher books are available for special promotions and premiums. For details contact: Special Markets Department, Macmillan, 175 Fifth Ave., New York, NY 10010.

For more information, please visit www.kingfisherbooks.com

Printed in China
10 9 8 7 6 5 4 3 2 1
1TR/0911/WKT/UNTD/140MA

The All About America series was produced for Kingfisher by Bender Richardson White, Uxbridge, U.K.
Editor: Lionel Bender
Designer: Ben White
DTP: Neil Sutton
Production: Kim Richardson
Consultant: Richard Jensen, Research Professor of History, Culver Stockton College, Missouri

Sources of quotations and excerpts
Page 12, famine quote: Daniels, Roger. *Coming to America*. New York: HarperCollins, 1990, page 130.
Page 13, job advertisement: Wills, Chuck, *Destination America*. New York: DK Publishing, 2005, page 145.
Page 15, Castle Garden quote: *New York Times* newspaper, December 26, 1866.
Page 17, Swedish and Norwegian immigrant quotes: Wills, Chuck. *Destination America*. New York: DK Publishing, 2005, pages 150, 151.
Page 18, farmer advertisement: *The Northwest*, Vol. I, No. 1, New York and St. Paul, January 15, 1883.
Page 19, Immigration Act excerpt: Immigration Act of 1882, "United States Immigration Law History," http://freepages.genealogy.rootsweb.ancestry.com/~splatsresearch/us_imm_law.htm
Page 22, Island of Hope quote: Brownstone, David M., Irene M. Franck, and Douglass L. Brownstone. *Island of Hope, Island of Tears*. New York: Barnes & Noble Publishing, 2000, page 149.
Pages 26, 27, Mondale and Truman quotes: Daniels, Roger. *Coming to America: A History of Immigration and Ethnicity in American Life*. New York: HarperCollins, 1990, pages 296, 301.

Acknowledgments
The publishers would like to thank the following illustrators for their contribution to this book: Mark Bergin, James Field, John James, and Gerald Wood. Map: Neil Sutton. Book cover design: Neal Cobourne.
Cover artwork: Chris Molan.
The publishers thank the following for supplying photos for this book: *b* = bottom, *c* = center, *l* = left, *t* = top, *m* = middle
© The Art Archive: page 9bl, 27tr (20th Century Fox/The Kobal Collection) • © The Bridgeman Art Library: pages 12 (The Stapleton Collection), 14 (Collection of the New-York Historical Society), 14 (Bourne Gallery, Reigate, Surrey, U.K.) • © CORBIS: pages 4tl (Warren Morgan) • © Getty Images: 5tr, 6tl, 26tl, 26bl (Gamma-Keystone), 27m • © iStockphoto: 4br (Ryerson Clark), 17 (Erik Lam), 20 (craftvision), 28tl (Laura Young), 28mr (Karen Mower), 29tl (Kirby Hamilton) • © Library of Congress: pages 1, 2–3, 30–31, 32 (LC-DIG-ggbain-03252), 19 (LC-DIG-ppmsca-17886) • © National Park Service: page 22 • © TopFoto.co.uk· The Granger Collection/TopFoto: cover, pages 1, 6rm, 9t, 9lc, 9bl, 9br, 10br, 11t, 11br, 12tl, 12bl, 13b, 15bl, 16–17, 17bl, 19c, 19bc, 20c, 20r, 20br, 21l, 22, 23tl, 23tr, 23br, 23bl, 24tl, 25t, 25cl, 24–25, 26–27, 28, 23 (ullsteinbild).
Every effort has been made to trace the copyright holders of the images. The publishers apologize for any omissions.

Note to readers: The website addresses listed in this book are correct at the time of publishing. However, due to the ever-changing nature of the Internet, website addresses and content can change. Websites can contain links that are unsuitable for children. The publisher cannot be held responsible for changes in website addresses or content or for information obtained through third-party websites. We strongly advise that Internet searches should be supervised by an adult.

CONTENTS

The First Peoples   4
European Immigrants   6
The Slaves' Journey   8
Migration Continues   10
A Better Life   12
Golden Dreams   14
The Lure of Land   16
Immigrants Move West   18
Mass Arrivals   20
Ellis Island   22
Settling in Cities   24
The World Wars   26
Toward Modern America   28
Glossary   30
Timeline   31
Information   31
Index   32

Introduction

Immigrants are people who enter a country to live there, having come from another country—their homeland. Even before the United States became a nation in 1776, a large percentage of the people living in its land had been immigrants. The first immigrants came from western Europe. They were soon followed by people from eastern Europe, China, and West Africa. Later, immigrants came from southern Europe, Canada, Central and South America, and Asia. The immigrants initially came mostly by sea but later overland and by air. They came to the United States to find freedom and better opportunities. Most of them succeeded in their dream. The story is presented as a series of double-page articles, each one looking at a particular period of U.S. history up to the present day. It is illustrated with paintings, engravings, and photographs from the times, mixed with artists' impressions of everyday scenes and situations.

The First Peoples

Spreading from far north to south

Most experts believe that the first people in North America walked from present-day Siberia to Alaska more than 12,000 years ago, when the regions were connected by land. From there, people spread gradually southward.

Today, there is a narrow stretch of ocean—the Bering Strait—between Siberia in Asia and Alaska in North America. But from 25,000 to 12,000 years ago, the world was colder than it is now. The sea level was lower because water was frozen in huge glaciers that covered the land. There was a wide land bridge called Beringia connecting Siberia and Alaska. Siberian hunters moved eastward into Beringia and later reached Alaska as they followed the animals they depended on for food.

The Siberian hunters probably arrived between 17,000 and 12,000 years ago. They were the first North American immigrants—people who come to live in a place different from their homeland. We learn about these people through spearheads, arrowheads, stone tools, carvings, and bones found at prehistoric sites.

▲ This large spearhead was used about 13,000 years ago by prehistoric hunters near modern-day Clovis, New Mexico. Some scientists believe the first people arrived in North America thousands of years before this.

Beringia

At times, Beringia was about 1,000 miles (1,600 km) wide, made up of grasslands that are now under the waters of the Bering Strait, Bering Sea, and Arctic Ocean. Hunters probably lived for many centuries in Beringia before moving on to Alaska.

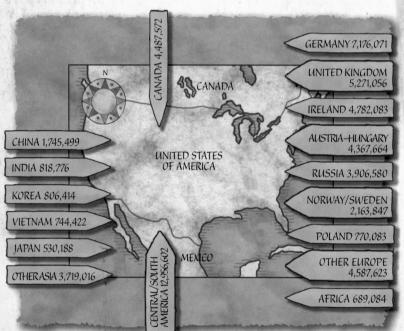

CANADA 4,487,572

GERMANY 7,176,071

UNITED KINGDOM 5,271,056

IRELAND 4,782,083

AUSTRIA–HUNGARY 4,367,664

RUSSIA 3,906,580

NORWAY/SWEDEN 2,163,847

POLAND 770,083

OTHER EUROPE 4,587,623

AFRICA 689,084

CHINA 1,745,499

INDIA 818,776

KOREA 806,414

VIETNAM 744,422

JAPAN 530,188

OTHER ASIA 3,719,016

CENTRAL/SOUTH AMERICA 12,956,602

N

CANADA

UNITED STATES OF AMERICA

MEXICO

▲ Numbers of immigrants entering the United States from 1820 to 2000, grouped by home country or region of the world

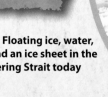

▶ Floating ice, water, and an ice sheet in the Bering Strait today

Arctic People

Today, there are two native groups living in the far north of America: the Inuit and the Yupik. They also came from Siberia but arrived thousands of years later than the first immigrants.

Big Game Hunting

The first Americans hunted big mammals such as mammoths, mastodons, giant bison, camels, horses, and tapirs. Most of these big mammals became extinct from 13,000 to 10,000 years ago, around the time the glaciers melted.

▲ A Yupik man living on Nunivak Island in Alaska prepares his sealskin kayak to go fishing or seal hunting.

Populating America

At the time the first people reached Alaska, two great ice sheets covered much of North America. From 14,000 to 12,000 years ago, the ice sheets began to melt, opening a path between them that allowed people to move south toward the Great Plains. Even earlier, people may have moved down the west coast—which was not covered by ice—by land, small boats, or both. Other routes may have been used as well.

The remains of ancient settlements have been found throughout North and South America, including in Virginia, Mexico, and Chile. For thousands of years, people continued to move in search of food and better land. They developed into the many American Indian tribes that Europeans met when they first came to America.

5

European Immigrants
The first settlements in today's United States

The first European immigrants to the New World sailed across the Atlantic Ocean to the east coast of the Americas. They were looking for new opportunities, riches, adventure, and freedom—as were the many pioneers and settlers who followed them.

▲ The first European immigrants found a land full of native people. This 1634 engraving shows English settlers meeting American Indians on a bank of the Potomac River in present-day Virginia.

In about A.D. 1000, a small group of Vikings sailed from Greenland to the east coast of present-day Canada and spent the winter at a place they called Vinland. About ten years later, some 160 Viking settlers arrived in the same region. They left after three years, when the local people became hostile, but they were the first Europeans who tried to live in North America.

Almost 500 years later, in 1492, Christopher Columbus landed on an island in the Caribbean Sea and claimed the land for Spain. He was looking for a new sea route to India, but when his men discovered that the native people had gold, more Spanish explorers sailed to North and South America. Soon other Europeans came from England, France, the Netherlands, and Sweden.

Spanish Immigrants

The Spanish settled first on the islands of the Caribbean Sea and then set up a permanent capital in Mexico City, Mexico, in 1519. From the Caribbean, they moved north into Florida. From Mexico, they moved north into New Mexico and later into Texas and California.

▶ A Catholic church built by the Spanish in a Mexican village

▲ The Vikings were great sailors with well-made ships. They originally came from Norway, Sweden, and Denmark.

The French Settle

By the late 1500s, the French had established fur-trading posts along the St. Lawrence River in Canada. During the next 125 years, the French spread through the Great Lakes region and Mississippi River valley south to New Orleans, which they founded in 1718.

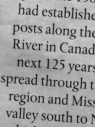

Pilgrims prepare to sail from England on the *Mayflower* in September 1620.

Permanent places to live

The early European immigrants lived in colonies under rules approved by their home countries. Each colony was more than a fort or a trading post; it was a new place to live. The first permanent colony was established by the Spanish at St. Augustine, Florida, in 1565. In 1592, about 500 people, including men, women, children, and American Indian slaves, traveled north from Mexico and settled in what is now New Mexico.

The English established their first successful colony when 104 men and boys settled at Jamestown, Virginia, in 1607. (The first English women did not arrive until 1619.) By 1732, there were 13 British colonies along the east coast. The first permanent French colony was founded at Quebec, Canada, in 1608. The Dutch set up their first permanent settlement on an island near Manhattan, New York, in 1624 and bought Manhattan from the Lenape Indians two years later. The Swedes settled near Wilmington, Delaware, in 1638.

Pilgrims and Puritans

Some early English immigrants came to North America looking for a place to practice their religion without interference. Beginning with the landing of the *Mayflower* at Plymouth in December 1620, a few hundred members of a religious group, called the Pilgrims, settled in Massachusetts. From 1630 to 1640, they were followed by about 20,000 Puritans, who founded the Massachusetts Bay Colony.

An English tobacco plantation with black workers in about 1670. The workers were treated at first as servants but later as slaves.

The Slaves' Journey
Workers on plantations and large farms

When European farmers in America needed workers to help in their fields, a new type of immigration began. African people were taken by force from their homeland and brought across the Atlantic Ocean to work as slaves.

▲ Slaves being sold at auction

▼ A slave family in about 1800, in the southern United States, cooking a meal in their slave quarters on a plantation. Slaves developed their own culture in the South.

In 1619, a Swedish ship arrived in Jamestown, Virginia, with about 20 Africans. The English farmers traded food in exchange for the Africans, who were put to work in their tobacco fields. At first, most of these Africans and those who followed were treated as indentured servants, which meant that they could earn their freedom after working for a certain period. There were also many white indentured servants from Europe who worked to pay for their transportation to America.

Gradually, the laws changed for Africans. In 1705, the Virginia government stated that all non-Christians (including Africans) who were brought into the country would be considered slaves. They could be bought and sold by their owners and made to work without pay. Some American Indians were also made slaves.

Slave Families

American law did not recognize slave marriages and families. Husbands, wives, and children could be sold to different owners at any time. Despite this, many slave families stayed together, and many who were separated maintained strong family bonds.

An Awful Trade

Slavery became known as the Triangle Trade. On the first leg of the triangle, European ships carried trade goods to West Africa to exchange for slaves. The slaves were black people usually captured in wars by other Africans. Then, in the "middle passage," the ships carried the slaves from West Africa to be sold in the New World—the Americas. Finally, the ships returned to Europe with sugar, tobacco, and rum to sell.

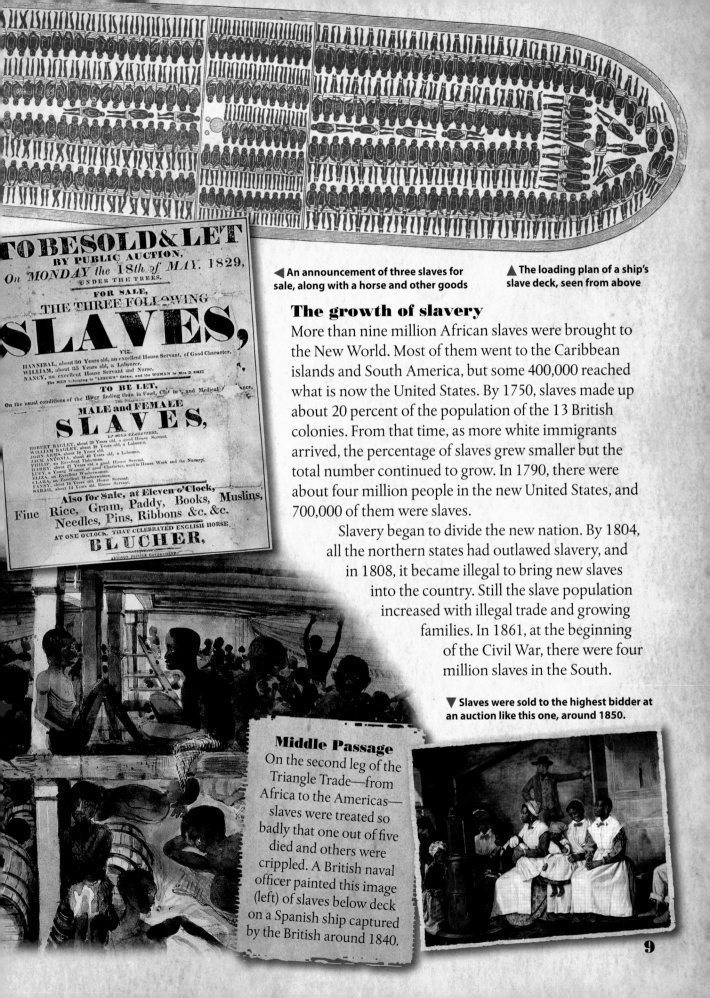

◄ An announcement of three slaves for sale, along with a horse and other goods

▲ The loading plan of a ship's slave deck, seen from above

The growth of slavery

More than nine million African slaves were brought to the New World. Most of them went to the Caribbean islands and South America, but some 400,000 reached what is now the United States. By 1750, slaves made up about 20 percent of the population of the 13 British colonies. From that time, as more white immigrants arrived, the percentage of slaves grew smaller but the total number continued to grow. In 1790, there were about four million people in the new United States, and 700,000 of them were slaves.

Slavery began to divide the new nation. By 1804, all the northern states had outlawed slavery, and in 1808, it became illegal to bring new slaves into the country. Still the slave population increased with illegal trade and growing families. In 1861, at the beginning of the Civil War, there were four million slaves in the South.

▼ Slaves were sold to the highest bidder at an auction like this one, around 1850.

Middle Passage

On the second leg of the Triangle Trade—from Africa to the Americas—slaves were treated so badly that one out of five died and others were crippled. A British naval officer painted this image (left) of slaves below deck on a Spanish ship captured by the British around 1840.

9

Migration Continues

By 1840, the population reaches 17 million

After the first European immigrants established colonies, the number of people in North America grew much faster than in Europe. Some of this growth was due to immigration, but most of it came from children who were born in the new land.

Throughout much of U.S. history, from 10 to 15 percent of the country's people have been immigrants, a trend that has continued to the present day. However, during the American Revolution (1775–1783), the War of 1812 (1812–1815), and a series of subsequent wars in Europe, immigration slowed to a trickle so that, by 1815, almost 99 percent of U.S. citizens were native-born. That began to change with the end of these wars. In 1820, the U.S. government counted immigrants for the first time. During the next 20 years, almost 750,000 new Americans arrived—the beginning of a great new wave of immigration.

Spanish America

The Spanish first settled in Florida and New Mexico and then in Texas and California. They built Catholic missions for the Indians, *presidios* (forts) for soldiers, and towns for settlers. The Spanish struggled to attract settlers to these colonies that were far from Mexico City, the capital of New Spain. Land-hungry U.S. citizens were eager to expand their growing nation into the Spanish possessions.

▶ Spanish soldiers escort California Indian workers back to the mission buildings.

From Forts to Cities

Many U.S. cities began as forts built by Europeans to protect the frontiers of their colonies. Pittsburgh, Pennsylvania, for example, grew on a site where the French and British both built forts during the French and Indian War (1754–1763). The French Fort Detroit, built in 1701, became the city of Detroit, Michigan.

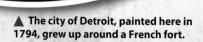

▲ The city of Detroit, painted here in 1794, grew up around a French fort.

Highland Clearances

Around 1760, landlords in the highlands of Scotland began to clear, or force, small farmers off their land. The price of wool was high, and the landlords could make more money by raising flocks of sheep on the land. Many of the small farmers emigrated to North America, Australia, and New Zealand. The first large migration was in 1792, known as the Year of the Sheep.

◀ **In 1763, Great Britain took Canada from the French. These British people are bound for Canada around 1830 to escape the bad living conditions at home.**

The Scotch-Irish

By 1700, many Scottish people had settled in Northern Ireland. Known as the Scotch-Irish, they were the first large group of non-English immigrants in British America. From 1717 to 1770, about 250,000 arrived. By the time they arrived, most of the good land along the east coast was already taken. Some settled in cities, but most pushed westward into the wilderness. They were pioneers, settling in the Appalachian Mountains region of the original colonies and eventually in new states such as Kentucky and Ohio.

A Two-Way Exchange

During the American Revolution, around 500,000 white people in the British colonies remained loyal to Britain. Most Loyalists stayed in the United States, but about 80,000 left for Canada or Britain. This illustration (right) shows a Loyalist family heading north to Canada. This was the first time that a large group of people moved away from the United States. However, at this time the number of U.S. immigrants—Scotch-Irish, English, French, Dutch, German—was far greater.

A Better Life

Cities swell as immigrants flood in

Between 1841 and 1860, more than four million people came to the United States to escape famine, revolutions, and changing economies in Europe. By far, most of these immigrants—four out of every five—were Irish or German.

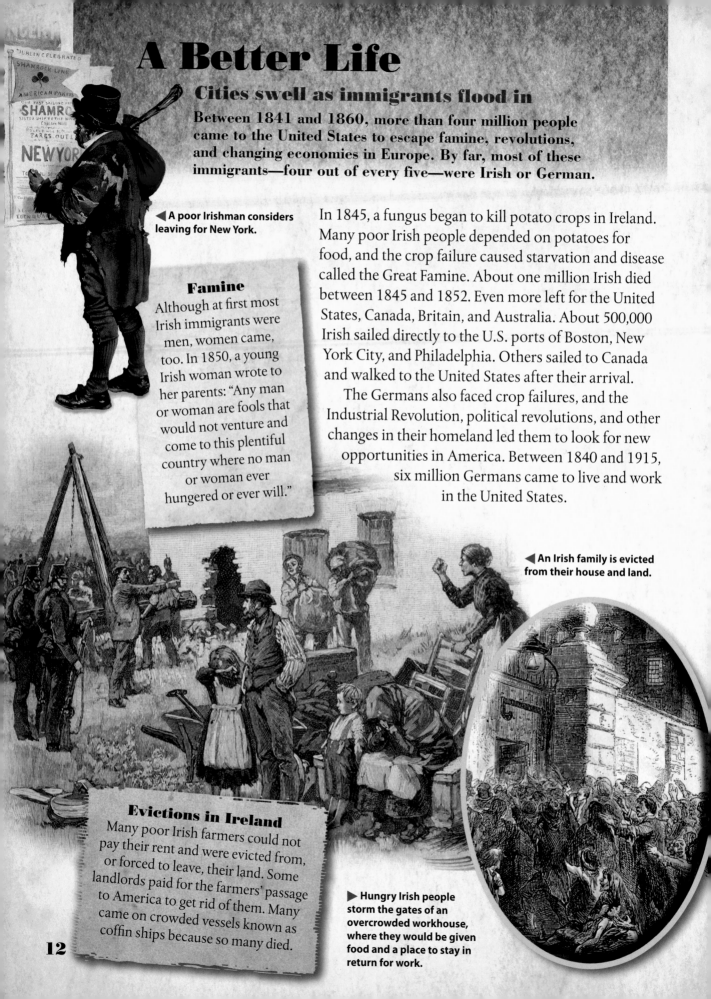

◀ A poor Irishman considers leaving for New York.

Famine

Although at first most Irish immigrants were men, women came, too. In 1850, a young Irish woman wrote to her parents: "Any man or woman are fools that would not venture and come to this plentiful country where no man or woman ever hungered or ever will."

In 1845, a fungus began to kill potato crops in Ireland. Many poor Irish people depended on potatoes for food, and the crop failure caused starvation and disease called the Great Famine. About one million Irish died between 1845 and 1852. Even more left for the United States, Canada, Britain, and Australia. About 500,000 Irish sailed directly to the U.S. ports of Boston, New York City, and Philadelphia. Others sailed to Canada and walked to the United States after their arrival.

The Germans also faced crop failures, and the Industrial Revolution, political revolutions, and other changes in their homeland led them to look for new opportunities in America. Between 1840 and 1915, six million Germans came to live and work in the United States.

◀ An Irish family is evicted from their house and land.

Evictions in Ireland

Many poor Irish farmers could not pay their rent and were evicted from, or forced to leave, their land. Some landlords paid for the farmers' passage to America to get rid of them. Many came on crowded vessels known as coffin ships because so many died.

▶ Hungry Irish people storm the gates of an overcrowded workhouse, where they would be given food and a place to stay in return for work.

◀ Soldiers helped landlords evict poor people from their homes in western Ireland during the Great Famine.

Immigrant Families

Most German immigrants arrived with their families and had enough money to make a start in the United States. Many settled on farms or in smaller towns, while others settled in cities as businessmen and skilled workers. The Irish were poorer, and most of them settled in big cities, where they took less-skilled jobs. During the Great Famine, they often brought their families in stages, with one family member working and sending money back to Ireland for another to follow.

Anti-immigrant attitudes

Although Irish and German immigrants had come to the United States since before the American Revolution, the arrival of so many in such a short time disturbed some native-born Americans. The Irish were mostly Catholic, while most U.S. citizens were Protestants who did not trust the Pope and the Roman Catholic Church. In big cities where the Irish settled, job advertisements often read: "No Irish need apply." Many Germans were also Catholic, and they did not speak English, making them unpopular. These anti-immigrant feelings weakened during the Civil War but did not disappear.

▲ Irish people wait to board a ship to America at the port city of Cork, Ireland, in this 1851 engraving.

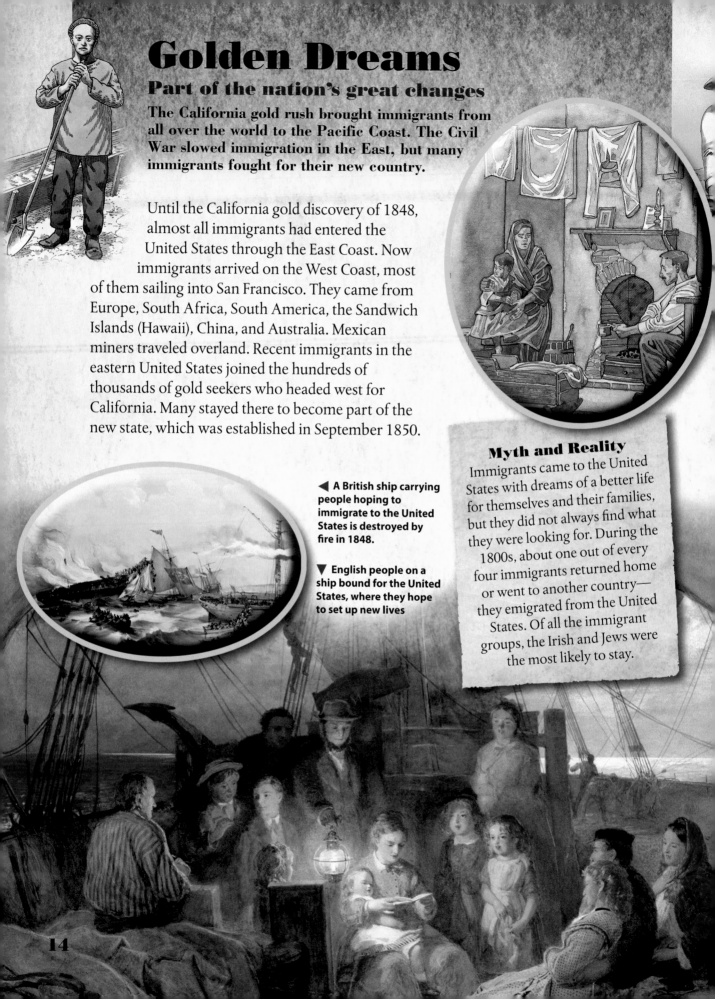

Golden Dreams

Part of the nation's great changes

The California gold rush brought immigrants from all over the world to the Pacific Coast. The Civil War slowed immigration in the East, but many immigrants fought for their new country.

Until the California gold discovery of 1848, almost all immigrants had entered the United States through the East Coast. Now immigrants arrived on the West Coast, most of them sailing into San Francisco. They came from Europe, South Africa, South America, the Sandwich Islands (Hawaii), China, and Australia. Mexican miners traveled overland. Recent immigrants in the eastern United States joined the hundreds of thousands of gold seekers who headed west for California. Many stayed there to become part of the new state, which was established in September 1850.

◀ **A British ship carrying people hoping to immigrate to the United States is destroyed by fire in 1848.**

▼ **English people on a ship bound for the United States, where they hope to set up new lives**

Myth and Reality

Immigrants came to the United States with dreams of a better life for themselves and their families, but they did not always find what they were looking for. During the 1800s, about one out of every four immigrants returned home or went to another country— they emigrated from the United States. Of all the immigrant groups, the Irish and Jews were the most likely to stay.

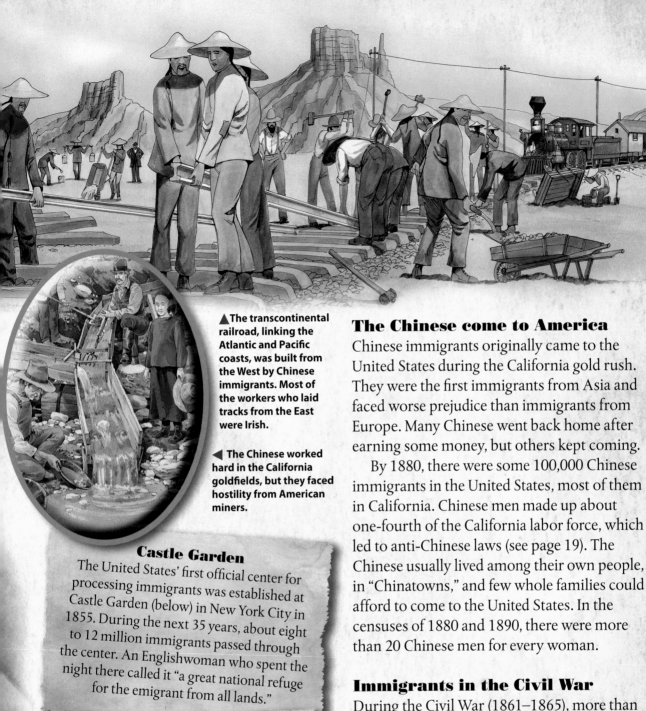

▲ The transcontinental railroad, linking the Atlantic and Pacific coasts, was built from the West by Chinese immigrants. Most of the workers who laid tracks from the East were Irish.

◄ The Chinese worked hard in the California goldfields, but they faced hostility from American miners.

Castle Garden

The United States' first official center for processing immigrants was established at Castle Garden (below) in New York City in 1855. During the next 35 years, about eight to 12 million immigrants passed through the center. An Englishwoman who spent the night there called it "a great national refuge for the emigrant from all lands."

The Chinese come to America

Chinese immigrants originally came to the United States during the California gold rush. They were the first immigrants from Asia and faced worse prejudice than immigrants from Europe. Many Chinese went back home after earning some money, but others kept coming.

By 1880, there were some 100,000 Chinese immigrants in the United States, most of them in California. Chinese men made up about one-fourth of the California labor force, which led to anti-Chinese laws (see page 19). The Chinese usually lived among their own people, in "Chinatowns," and few whole families could afford to come to the United States. In the censuses of 1880 and 1890, there were more than 20 Chinese men for every woman.

Immigrants in the Civil War

During the Civil War (1861–1865), more than 500,000 immigrants served in the Union army—about one out of every four soldiers. Most of them were German and Irish, but there were men from every nationality. Some volunteered to show their support for their new country, others were drafted, and still others served as paid replacements for men who did not want to fight. Immigrants also fought for the Confederacy.

The Lure of Land

Setting up farms in the Midwest

After the Civil War, people in the United States, including immigrants, looked for opportunities west of the Mississippi River. New land opened as the army forced the American Indians onto reservations—land set aside for them.

During the late 1800s, many more immigrants settled in cities than on farms. But those who did work the land played an important role in the nation's westward movement. They included families who owned their farms and laborers who worked for them.

The Scandinavians

About two million people from Scandinavia (Sweden, Norway, Denmark, and Iceland) came to the United States between the end of the Civil War and 1920. The Scandinavian countries had little land for farming, so many immigrant farmers settled in northern midwestern states, including Illinois, Wisconsin, Minnesota, Iowa, Nebraska, and the Dakotas. Other Scandinavians settled in midwestern cities.

The Homestead Act

In 1862, the U.S. Congress passed the Homestead Act, which offered 160 acres (65 hectares) of government land in the West free to anyone who met certain conditions. Immigrants could claim land as long as they planned to become U.S. citizens. This brought a new wave of immigration. All homesteaders, whether native-born or immigrant, had to "improve the land" within six months and live on it for five years. Less than half succeeded, but those who did achieved the American dream of owning land and working for themselves.

▼ Sod buildings were a quick way to provide shelter and storage. Farmers replaced them with wood buildings as soon as they could afford to buy the materials.

▲ A pioneer family sits in front of their sod house on the plains in the late 1800s.

Prairies and plains

Most immigrants who settled on western lands after the Civil War were from Germany or Scandinavia. There were also Canadians, British, Swiss, and, later, eastern Europeans. For the Scandinavians, the cold climate of the northern Midwest was similar to the climate of their native countries. Even so, it was a difficult challenge. An early Swedish immigrant told a reporter: "None who are not accustomed to hard agricultural labor ought to become farmers in this country."

Farming was difficult enough in prairie states such as Illinois, Wisconsin, Minnesota, and Iowa, where there was enough rainfall, tall grass, and trees. It became much more difficult as farmers were forced to move farther west into the Great Plains of Kansas, Nebraska, and the Dakotas, where there was little rainfall, short grass, few trees, and powerful winds. Still, native-born and immigrant families alike succeeded.

◀ After the Civil War, almost all immigrants traveled on steamships instead of the slower sailing ships.

American Fever

Immigrants who went back to visit their homeland often persuaded others to join them in the United States. In 1871, a Norwegian woman wrote that a visiting villager "infected half the population in that district with what was called the American fever . . . It was like a desperate case of homesickness reversed."

▼ Everyone in a farming family had to help with the chores in order to succeed.

Sod Houses

On the treeless plains, pioneers built houses out of sod—the top layer of earth, including grass, roots, and dirt. Using a plow with a sharp, curved steel blade, they cut the sod into bricks and placed them with the roots up so they would grow into one another.

Immigrants Move West
Anti-immigrant feelings grow stronger

The western railroads inspired many European immigrants to settle on land in the American West. At the same time, there were new efforts to keep Chinese immigrants out.

To help pay for the cost of building railroads in the West, the U.S. government gave the railroad companies large areas of land along the tracks. The government wanted to sell this land, and it wanted to encourage settlers to move west so they could produce crops, livestock, and other goods for the railroads to ship to other parts of the country.

The railroad companies set up travel offices in the East and in northern Europe and sent out pamphlets advertising opportunities for farmers. Railroads and steamship companies offered package deals that allowed immigrants to travel straight from Europe to their new land. Advertisements were often exaggerated, and immigrants who bought land without seeing it were often disappointed. Many others were excited to own more land than they could ever have owned in Europe.

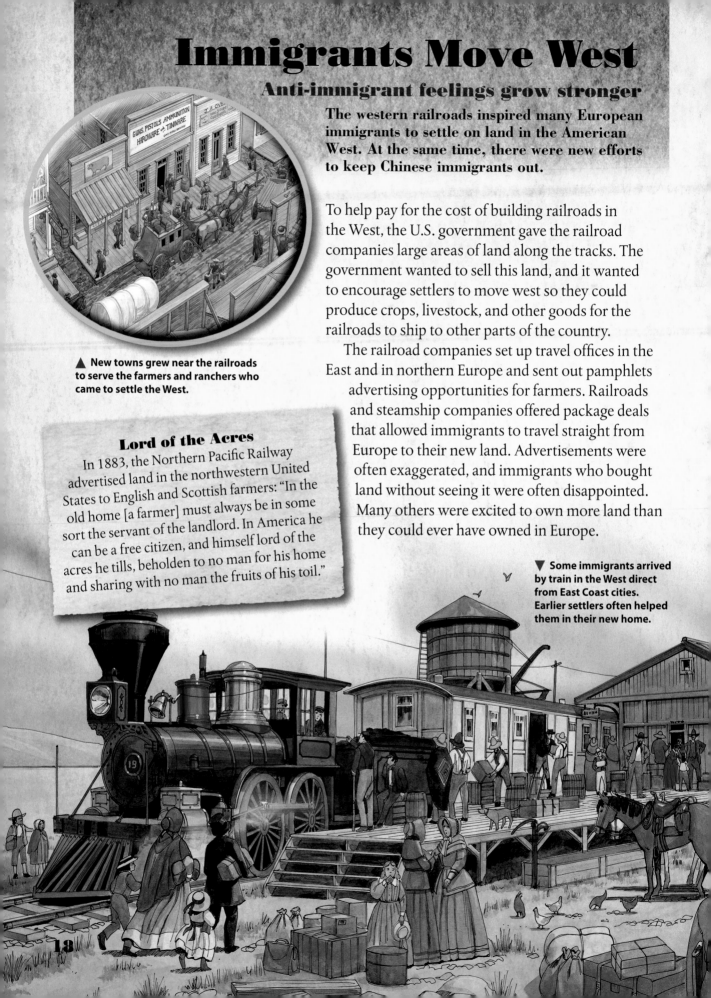

▲ New towns grew near the railroads to serve the farmers and ranchers who came to settle the West.

Lord of the Acres

In 1883, the Northern Pacific Railway advertised land in the northwestern United States to English and Scottish farmers: "In the old home [a farmer] must always be in some sort the servant of the landlord. In America he can be a free citizen, and himself lord of the acres he tills, beholden to no man for his home and sharing with no man the fruits of his toil."

▼ Some immigrants arrived by train in the West direct from East Coast cities. Earlier settlers often helped them in their new home.

◀ "The Chinese Must Go," proclaims this advertisement.

▲ Chinese immigrants photographed in 1902

Immigration laws

Anti-Chinese feelings increased as more people settled in the West. The Chinese worked for low wages, and Americans believed they took jobs from U.S. and European immigrant workers. In 1882, Congress passed the Chinese Exclusion Act, which prohibited Chinese from becoming citizens and stopped immigration from China for ten years. The Act was later renewed and stayed in force until 1943.

Another 1882 law established a tax of 50¢ ($11 by today's value) on each immigrant to help pay for government services and prohibited immigration for any "convict, lunatic, idiot or person unable to take care of himself or herself without becoming a public charge."

▲ Uncle Sam welcomes immigrants to the "U.S. Ark of Refuge [safety]."

The Right Type of Immigrant
The United States of America usually welcomed white, English-speaking, Protestant immigrants and often resisted those who did not have white skin, spoke a different language, or practiced a different religion. Who was the right type of immigrant? The debate grew more intense when jobs became scarce during the depression of the 1890s.

Mass Arrivals

New languages and cultures

Between 1881 and 1924, almost 26 million immigrants came to the United States, an average of about 600,000 each year. This mass immigration required new responses by the U.S. government.

Except for African slaves and the Chinese, almost all immigrants before 1880 had come from northern and western Europe. After that, new immigrants arrived from southern and eastern European countries such as Italy, Greece, Poland, Croatia, Hungary, Czechoslovakia, and Russia.

The Industrial Revolution had changed the economies of these countries, forcing many rural people to leave their farms and look for work in big cities, at first in Europe and later in the United States. Others left their native countries to avoid being forced into the army. Russian and eastern European Jews fled brutal religious persecution. The new immigrants did not blend quickly into American society, but in time they, too, would become U.S. citizens.

▲ Trunks and baskets used by immigrants to carry their belongings

▼ Steerage passengers heading from Antwerp, Belgium, to New York City in about 1893 crowd together on deck to breathe fresh air.

▶ Steamship ticket for a family of four Polish immigrants from Hamburg, Germany, to New York City in October 1913

Traveling Steerage

Big steamships offered wealthy passengers comfortable cabins, but most immigrants traveled in crowded quarters called steerage, located on a lower deck. Here hundreds of passengers ate together, fought seasickness, and slept on bunk beds stacked two or three high within separate compartments for single men, single women, and families.

▶ This landing card, from 1923, was a form of identification presented by an immigrant to immigration officials upon arriving in the United States.

The Statue of Liberty

The Statue of Liberty was dedicated in 1886 as a gift from the people of France. It became a symbol of freedom for millions of immigrants who passed through New York Harbor.

▲ Steamships cut travel time from Europe to two weeks, compared with three months for sailing ships.

The Melting Pot

The United States has been called a melting pot because people from many cultures have "melted" together into one. Yet many U.S. citizens from other countries have also kept their own culture. The term "melting pot" comes from a play first produced in Washington, D.C., in 1908.

Limiting the number of immigrants

The mass arrivals that began in the 1880s led to stricter immigration control. The Immigration Act of 1917 barred many immigrants with a physical or mental illness, raised the tax on each immigrant to $8 ($136 by today's value), and required adults to read at least 40 words in their own language. It also barred immigrants from most of Asia except for the Philippines, which was then a U.S. possession, and Japan, which had a special agreement with the United States.

In 1924, a new law restricted the total number of immigrants to 150,000 each year using a "quota system" that limited the number of immigrants from any country to 2 percent of the people from that country already living in the United States, as counted in the 1890 census. This reduced the number who could come from southern or eastern Europe.

21

Ellis Island

Checked before entering the country

The massive wave of immigrants, most coming through the port of New York City, required a larger immigration center. Beginning in 1892, about 12 million immigrants passed through Ellis Island in New York Harbor.

▲ Badge from the cap of an immigration officer

▼ The Ellis Island immigration facility. For those immigrants sent home, it was the "Island of Tears."

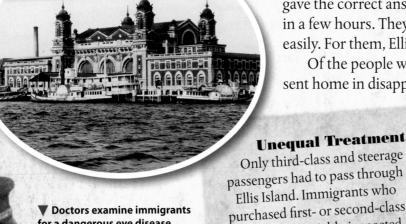

▼ Doctors examine immigrants for a dangerous eye disease, trachoma, which was common in southern and eastern Europe.

Ellis Island was the first immigration center run by the federal government. The old New York center, Castle Garden, had been run by the state and the city. As they passed through Ellis Island, immigrants were checked by doctors for various diseases, asked a series of legal questions, and tested for mental abilities if they seemed "feeble-minded." Those who were in good health and gave the correct answers could pass through the center in a few hours. They entered the United States fairly easily. For them, Ellis Island was the "Island of Hope."

Of the people with problems, about 2 percent were sent home in disappointment. After the quota system was established in 1924, most immigrants received visas in their home countries and did not have to pass through Ellis Island.

Unequal Treatment

Only third-class and steerage passengers had to pass through Ellis Island. Immigrants who purchased first- or second-class cabins were quickly inspected onboard the ship when it docked at the pier. Then they passed directly through U.S. Customs (to check their possessions). The government believed that immigrants who could afford more expensive passage were the least likely to be a problem for society.

◀ Immigrants look out at the Statue of Liberty in about 1920.

Passing the tests at Ellis Island center

As immigrants walked up the stairs into the Great Hall, doctors observed them for signs of lameness, trouble breathing, or other obvious problems. Next, doctors lifted the immigrants' eyelids with a buttonhook to check for an eye disease called trachoma. If they found a problem, the doctors marked the immigrants' clothing in chalk with a special symbol to indicate that further testing was needed. (Some immigrants wiped off the chalk marks.) When the medical exam was over, the immigrants moved on to legal inspectors, who—with help from interpreters—asked 29 questions concerning facts such as their name, marital status, occupation, and whether they had relatives in America.

The Literacy Test

Beginning in 1917, immigrants aged 16 and over were required to read at least 40 words in their native language. This was usually a passage from the Bible, as in the passage below in the Armeno-Turkish language. Although this test may seem simple by modern standards, it was controversial. Three different U.S. presidents—Grover Cleveland, William Taft, and Woodrow Wilson—blocked immigration laws containing a literacy test before it was approved by Congress.

▲ Immigrants eat lunch on the second floor of the Ellis Island center.

▼ A Belgian family fleeing from World War I arrives at Ellis Island in 1917.

2674   Armeno-Turkish

No. 5   Serial Number

His substance also was seven thousand sheep, and three thousand camels, and five hundred yoke of oxen, and five hundred she asses, and a very great household; so that this man was the greatest of all the men of the east.

(Job 1:3)

▲ An Ellis Island literacy test printed in Armeno-Turkish script (top) and in English, from about 1917

Settling in Cities
Packed into tenements

During the mass migration, most immigrants settled in big cities, where they often took low-paying jobs in factories. They made a great contribution to U.S. industry but faced a difficult life in the crowded cities.

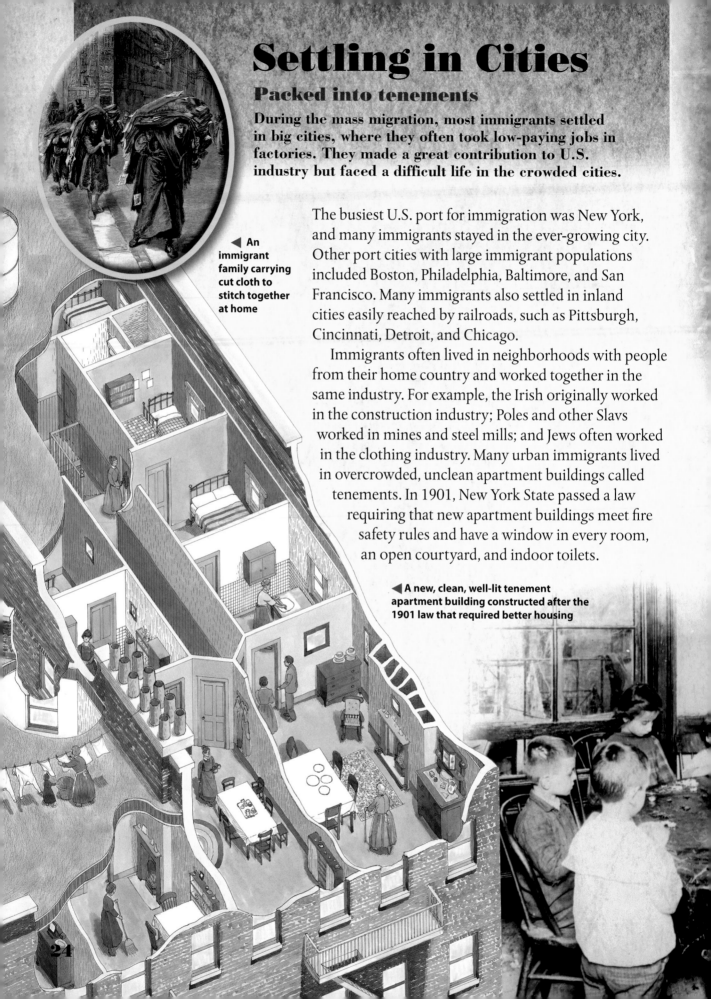

◀ An immigrant family carrying cut cloth to stitch together at home

The busiest U.S. port for immigration was New York, and many immigrants stayed in the ever-growing city. Other port cities with large immigrant populations included Boston, Philadelphia, Baltimore, and San Francisco. Many immigrants also settled in inland cities easily reached by railroads, such as Pittsburgh, Cincinnati, Detroit, and Chicago.

Immigrants often lived in neighborhoods with people from their home country and worked together in the same industry. For example, the Irish originally worked in the construction industry; Poles and other Slavs worked in mines and steel mills; and Jews often worked in the clothing industry. Many urban immigrants lived in overcrowded, unclean apartment buildings called tenements. In 1901, New York State passed a law requiring that new apartment buildings meet fire safety rules and have a window in every room, an open courtyard, and indoor toilets.

◀ A new, clean, well-lit tenement apartment building constructed after the 1901 law that required better housing

Immigrant City Life

Although many immigrants struggled with poverty, immigrant neighborhoods were exciting and colorful, combining customs of the home countries with a new life in the United States. In Chicago, there lived as many Poles and Swedes as there were in Warsaw and Stockholm, the capitals of Poland and Sweden, respectively.

HARPER'S WEEKLY.
JOURNAL OF CIVILIZATION.

Vol. XXXIII.—No. 1702.
Copyright, 1889, by Harper & Brothers.
All rights reserved.

NEW YORK, SATURDAY, AUGUST 10, 1889

TEN CENTS A COPY.
INCLUDING SUPPLEMENT.

Problems Bring Social Change

In 1890, a Danish immigrant named Jacob Riis published a book called *How the Other Half Lives*. Riis—who had been in the United States for 20 years—used his skills as a police reporter and the new technology of flash photography to show the terrible living conditions of immigrants in New York City. This book led to efforts to improve their conditions, including better medical care (shown on the magazine cover at left).

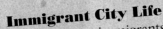

▲ The Lower East Side of Manhattan, shown here in 1905, was crowded with immigrants, including Irish, Italians, Poles, Greeks, and Jews.

From the boat to work

Many immigrants arrived with little money and needed to get jobs immediately to buy food and pay rent for housing. Often they were helped by people from their home country who had come before them and could speak both English and their native language. Sometimes these people were dishonest and took unfair advantage of the immigrants. Many immigrant children helped support their families by working in factories or mines or on the streets as performers and shoeshine boys.

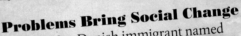

◀ A woman and her children making artificial flowers in their New York City tenement home, 1910

The World Wars

Decisions on citizens, aliens, and allies

Immigration practically stopped during the two world wars and the Great Depression of the 1930s. The wars forced U.S. citizens to face difficult questions about trusting immigrants from enemy countries.

שפּיין וועט געווינען דיא קריעג!
איהר קומט אהער צו געפינען פרייהייט.
יעצט מוזט איהר העלפען זיא צו בעשיצען
מיר מוזען דיא עלליים פֿערזארגען מיט ווייץ.
לאזט קיין זאך ניט גיין אין ניוועץ

יוניטעד סטייטס שפיין פערוואלטונג.

By the time the United States entered World War I in 1917, its people were already very concerned that immigration was out of control. (The Immigration Act, discussed on page 21, had been passed earlier that year.) During and after the war, a new law called the Espionage Act led to the arrest of thousands of German Americans and others who were suspected of being against the war or of supporting communism, socialism, or other beliefs that the U.S. government did not approve of. Many of these "enemy aliens" were brought to Ellis Island to be dealt with.

Immigration increased again during the 1920s, but the quota system slowed it down. During the 1930s, as the nation struggled with the Great Depression, immigration dropped to its lowest point since the 1830s. Between 1932 and 1935, more people left the country than arrived. World War II led to new efforts to control immigrants from Japan, Germany, and Italy.

Giving Support

During World War I, immigrants who did not fight in the U.S. Army were asked to help in other ways. This 1917 poster is written in Hebrew to appeal to Jewish immigrants. It reads: "Food will win the war! You came here seeking freedom, now you must help to preserve it. Wheat is needed for the allies. Waste nothing."

▶ **Japanese Americans are processed at a temporary camp at Santa Anita Racetrack, near Los Angeles, in April 1942.**

▲ **A group of German immigrants fleeing Nazi Germany arrive in 1939. They were among the few allowed into the United States.**

Escaping the Nazis

Before and during World War II, the United States made it very difficult for Jews and others to escape Nazi Germany and come to the country. Speaking of this time in 1979, Vice President Walter Mondale said that we "failed the test of civilization."

Enemy aliens and Japanese relocation

After the Japanese bombed Pearl Harbor, Hawaii, in December 1941, about one million immigrants of German, Japanese, and Italian descent were labeled "enemy aliens" and were watched closely by the government. More than 30,000 who had stated support for their homelands were arrested, and many others were kept in camps until the end of the war without knowing the charges against them. This program targeted only noncitizens, but their families —including citizens—often joined them. Later evidence indicates that few of these immigrants posed a threat.

In a separate program, about 110,000 people of Japanese descent, including citizens, were taken from their homes in the Pacific Coast region and relocated to camps.

An American Apology

Japanese Americans who were removed during World War II lost homes and businesses worth about $5 billion in today's value. In 1988, President Ronald Reagan signed a law apologizing for the removal and authorizing $20,000 to be paid to each survivor of the camps.

▶ *Gentleman's Agreement* won the Academy Award for best picture.

In the Movies

Although many Americans felt sympathy for the horrible treatment of Jews by the Nazis, anti-Jewish feelings (anti-Semitism) continued in the United States after the war. In the 1947 movie *Gentleman's Agreement*, a non-Jewish reporter pretends to be Jewish in order to discover the truth about anti-Semitism.

◀ Foreign women who married U.S. soldiers, such as these British "war brides," had special immigration status.

Displaced persons

Europeans forced from their countries by World War II became known as displaced persons (DPs). In 1947, President Truman asked Congress to "find ways whereby we can fulfill our responsibilities to these suffering and homeless refugees of all faiths." Many Americans did not agree that the United States had this responsibility, but Congress passed the Displaced Persons Act in 1948 and, by 1952, about 450,000 DPs had been let into the country.

Toward Modern America

The continuing search for the dream

U.S. immigration changed greatly after World War II. New immigration laws changed the rules, and more immigrants came from Latin America and Asia. Illegal immigration became a big concern, causing new anti-immigrant feelings.

The Border Patrol protects the nation's borders.

During the 1950s, many immigrants were deported (forced to leave the United States) because they were suspected of being communists. These men waved goodbye in 1952.

Since the end of World War II, the United States has struggled to control immigration while still being fair to the millions of people who want to come to the country. In 1952, a new law opened the door to all countries, beginning a flood of immigrants from Asia. (The ban on Chinese immigrants had been dropped during the war because China was a U.S. ally.)

The quota system for each country was dropped in 1965 and replaced by larger quotas for the "Old World" (Europe, Asia, and Africa) and "New World" (North and South America). Recent laws have allowed more legal immigrants and refugees while also preventing illegal immigration. About 40 million immigrants entered the United States legally between 1950 and 2010.

Migrant workers are often mistreated and paid very low wages. Founded in the 1960s, the United Farm Workers (UFW) union has fought for higher wages and better conditions for migrant workers.

LIBERTY

ELLIS ISLAND GATEWAY TO AMERICA

IN GOD WE TRUST

S

1986

Illegal Immigration

As of 2009, the Department of Homeland Security estimates that there are about 11 million illegal or "undocumented" immigrants in the United States. More than 60 percent are natives of Mexico, and many others come from Central or South America. Like most immigrants, they have come looking for better opportunities.

This silver dollar was issued in 1986, the 100th anniversary of the Statue of Liberty. Today, you can visit the statue and the immigration museum at Ellis Island center.

CALIFO 3 IFR 30

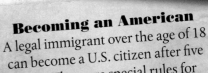

US CITIZENSHIP APPLICATION

Migrant Workers

Migrant workers move from place to place to work at low-paying farming jobs. In the United States, they historically have come from many immigrant groups as well as native-born families, but today, most U.S. migrant workers are Mexican. Although many are in the United States legally, there are also many illegal immigrants. Many farmers depend on this cheap source of labor and have resisted efforts to control the flow of illegal migrant workers.

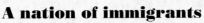

▲ A U.S. citizenship application form, the first step in the process of becoming an American citizen

Becoming an American

A legal immigrant over the age of 18 can become a U.S. citizen after five years. There are special rules for children. Here, eight-year-old Jenny Ye from China shows her U.S. citizenship certificate alongside the national flag after an official ceremony in Los Angeles.

A nation of immigrants

In 2010, about 310 million people lived in the United States, and almost 40 million of them were born in other countries. All of the rest—except for American Indians—are the descendants of post-1500 immigrants.

More than any country in the world, the United States is a nation of immigrants. At first, immigrants came mostly from Britain, then from the rest of northern Europe, and next from southern and eastern Europe. Today, Europeans make up less than 10 percent of immigrants, and most of the rest come from Latin America and Asia. Africans, Irish, Germans, Italians, Poles, Jews, Chinese, Japanese, and many others have overcome discrimination to become U.S. citizens and make great contributions to their adopted country. The immigrants of today are following the same path as those who came before them in search of the American dream of freedom and the chance for a better life.

29

Glossary

alien a person from another country who is not yet a citizen; a foreigner

allies in war, countries fighting on your side against common enemies

anti-Semitism negative attitudes and discrimination against Jewish people

Beringia a wide bridge of land that once connected Siberia and Alaska

census an official count of the number of people (the population) of a country

citizen a person who is a legal member of a country

colony an area in one country controlled by another country

communist a political system in which all businesses and land belong to the government and the profits are shared by everyone

customs a government agency responsible for inspecting goods brought into a country and for collecting appropriate fees and taxes

emigrant a person who leaves his or her homeland to live in another country

espionage spying or giving away secrets

eviction forcing a person to move out of the place where he or she lives

famine a time when a large number of people do not have enough to eat

homeland the country an immigrant comes from

illegal against the law

immigrant a person who enters a country to live permanently, having come from a different country—his or her homeland

indentured servant a person who must work for another person for a certain length of time to earn his or her freedom

lunatic a person with a mental illness; no longer used in official documents

mission a church and other buildings where American Indians were taught about Christianity; the Indians often lived and worked at the mission

New World North and South America, as opposed to the Old World of Europe, Asia, and Africa

pioneer a person who goes before others to start a new settlement

quota a certain number or percentage of people who are allowed into a country

refugee a person who flees a country to find safety or protection

settlement a place where people live, usually a homestead, village, or town

slave a person who is the property of another and is often made to work without pay for that person

steerage an area on the lower deck of a ship where passengers who bought the cheapest tickets traveled under crowded conditions

tenement a building divided into separate apartments that is usually poorly maintained and overcrowded

trachoma a bacterial infection of the eyes that can cause blindness if not treated

Vikings people from Norway, Sweden, and Denmark who raided and settled throughout the North Atlantic region between A.D. 700 and A.D. 1000; also called Norsemen

visa official document granting permission to enter a country

workhouse a place where poor people are taken care of in return for work

Timeline

about 1000 Vikings are the first Europeans to settle (briefly) in North America

1492 Christopher Columbus lands in the Caribbean islands and discovers America

1607 First permanent English settlement established at Jamestown

1619 First African slaves brought to America

1808 The importation of slaves into the United States is banned but continues illegally

1840s Crop failures and economic and political changes in Europe create mass immigration

1848 About 80,000 Mexican residents of the Southwest become U.S. citizens at the end of the Mexican War; the California gold discovery spurs immigration to the West Coast, including Chinese

1855 First official immigration center established at Castle Garden in New York Harbor

1862 The Homestead Act encourages immigration to the West

1880s Massive immigration begins, with almost 26 million immigrants between 1881 and 1924

1892 Ellis Island opens; serves as processing center for 12 million immigrants, most of them by 1924

1917 Immigration Act sets tests, taxes, and health checks to limit the number of immigrants

1924 National Origins Act sets a quota system and requires immigrants to get visas prior to entering the country, ending importance of Ellis Island

1940 The Alien Registration Act requires registration and fingerprinting of all aliens over the age of 14

1948 Displaced Persons Act allows many homeless Europeans to enter the United States

1952 Immigration and Nationality Act allows immigrants of all nations under a quota system

1954 Ellis Island closes

1965 National origins quota system repealed and priority given to family members of immigrants already in the United States

1986 About three million undocumented residents (illegal immigrants) allowed to stay

1996 Border enforcement strengthened

Information

WEBSITES

The Battery Conservancy (Castle Garden center)
www.castlegarden.org/
Statue of Liberty–Ellis Island Foundation
www.ellisisland.org/
Ellis Island, National Park Service
www.nps.gov/elis/index.htm
Gjenvick-Gjønvik Archives: Historical Immigration, Documents, Articles, and Other Immigration Items
www.gjenvick.com/Immigration/index.html
Homestead National Monument
www.nps.gov/home/index.htm
Oracle ThinkQuest: Immigration
http://library.thinkquest.org/20619/
Statue of Liberty National Monument
www.nps.gov/stli/index.htm

BOOKS TO READ

Bausum, Ann. *Denied, Detained, Deported: Stories from the Dark Side of American Immigration*. Washington, DC: National Geographic Children's Books, 2009.

Bial, Raymond. *Tenement: Immigrant Life on the Lower East Side*. Boston: Houghton Mifflin, 2002.

Haugen, David M., Susan Musser, and Kacy Lovelace, editors. *Immigration (Opposing Viewpoints)*. Detroit: Greenhaven Press, 2009.

Hoobler, Dorothy, and Thomas Hoobler. *We Are Americans: Voices of the Immigrant Experience*. New York: Scholastic, 2003.

Ollhoff, Jim. *Exploring Immigration (Your Family Tree)*. Edina, MN: ABDO & Daughters, 2010.

Rappaport, Doreen. Illustrated by Matt Tavares. *Lady Liberty: A Biography*. Cambridge, MA: Candlewick Press, 2008.

Sandler, Martin W. *Island of Hope: The Story of Ellis Island and the Journey to America*. New York: Scholastic, 2004.

Stefoff, Rebecca. *American Voices from a Century of Immigration: 1820–1924*. New York: Benchmark Books, 2006.

Index

Africa 3, 4, 8, 9, 14, 28
Alaska 4, 5
American Indians 5, 6, 8, 16
Asia 3, 15, 21, 28, 29
Atlantic Ocean 6, 8
Australia 11, 12, 14

Bering Strait 4
Britain 11, 12

California 6, 10, 14, 15
Canada 3, 6, 11, 12
Castle Garden 15, 22
Central and South America 3, 14, 28
children 7, 8, 10, 25, 29
China 3, 4, 14, 19, 29
Chinatown 15
cities 11, 12, 13, 16, 18, 24–25
Civil War 9, 13, 14, 15, 16, 17
coffin ships 12
colonies 7, 9, 10, 11

depression 19, 26
Detroit 10, 24

East Coast 7, 11, 14, 18
Ellis Island 22–23, 26, 28
Europe 3, 10, 12, 14, 15, 18, 20, 21,
    28, 29

farms and farming 8, 13, 16, 17, 18, 29
Florida 6, 7, 10
France 21

Germany 4, 17, 20, 26
gold 6, 14
Great Famine 12, 13
Great Plains 5, 17
Greece 20

Hawaii 14, 27

Homestead Act 16

immigrants 3, 4, 5, 9, 10, 12, 14, 15,
    16, 17, 18, 20, 21, 22, 23, 25, 26, 27,
    28, 29
immigrants, Chinese 15, 18, 19, 28
immigrants, eastern European 4, 17, 20,
    21, 22, 29
immigrants, English 7
immigrants, European 6, 10, 18, 19, 29
immigrants, German 13, 29
immigrants, Irish 12, 13, 29
Immigration Act 21, 26
Industrial Revolution 12
Inuit 5
Iowa 16, 17
Ireland 11, 12, 13
Italy 20, 26

Japan 4, 21, 26
Jews 14, 20, 24, 25, 26, 27, 29

Kentucky 11

landing cards 20
Literacy Test 23
Loyalists 11

Mayflower 7
Massachusetts 7
Mexico 5, 6, 7
Minnesota 16, 17
Mississippi River 6, 16

Nebraska 16, 17
New Mexico 4, 6, 7, 10
New Orleans 6,
New York 7, 12, 15, 20, 24, 25
New Zealand 11
North America 4, 5, 6, 7, 10
Norway 4

Ohio 11

Pacific Coast 14, 27
Philadelphia 12
Philippines 21
photographs 3, 19, 25
pioneers 6, 16
Pittsburg 10
plantations 7, 8
Poland 20, 25
puritans 7

railroads 15, 18
Russia 4, 20

San Francisco 14, 24
Scandinavia 16, 17
Scotland 11
settlers 6, 18
ships 6, 8, 13, 14, 17, 21
Siberia 4
slaves 7, 8, 9, 20
sod buildings 16, 17
Spanish 10
Statue of Liberty 21, 23, 28
steerage 20, 22
Sweden 4, 25

Texas 6, 10
Triangle Trade 8, 9

U.S. Congress 16, 19, 27
United States 3, 9, 11, 12, 13, 14, 15, 16,
    17, 19, 20, 21, 22, 25, 26, 27, 28, 29

Vikings 6
Vinland 4
Virginia 5, 6, 7, 8

women 7, 12, 15, 27
workhouses 12